GET WELL SOON !
ACTIVITY & PUZZLE
BOOK FOR MEN

CROSSWORDS, WORD FINDS, SUDOKU, INSPIRATIONAL QUOTE PUZZLES, FUN QUIZZES, JOKES AND TRIVIA

Wishing this book provides you a little fun and distraction and that you're feeling better soon!

FOOTBALL TEAMS CROSSWORD LOCATION TRIVIA

The clue describes the Teams Location. The answer is the Team name.

Across

5 The City that never sleeps
6 Volunteers
7 River City
8 Mile High City
11 Dogwood City
13 Charm City
16 Cigar City
18 City of Flowers and Sunshine
19 Tar Heel or Palmetto
20 The Magic City
23 Emerald City
25 The Crescent City
27 America's Finest City
28 Herds of animals almost made extinct in 1800's
29 Circle City

Down

1 Not a City or State
2 Golden Gate City
3 The Capital of the World
4 Windy City
9 Big D City
10 Mistake on the Lake
12 Full of Gophers
13 Bright side of the bay
14 Titletown USA
15 The Copper State
16 The Queen City
17 DMV
21 Motor City
22 Iron City
24 City of Brotherly Love
26 Clutch City

WORD FIND 1 - EARTH DAY

Acid Rain
All Natural
Bamboo
Carbon Neutral
Clean Air Act
Compost
Earth Day
Earth-friendly
Ecosystem
El Nino
Endangered
Extinct
Fertility
Flood
Forest
Mass Transit
Organic
Ozone Layer
Pesticide
Population
Radioactive
Recycle
Recycling
Sand Storm
Sewage
Smog
Sustainable
Tsunami

```
O Z O N E L A Y E R T I K J Y F M E W
S A N D S T O R M S T X V S O L Z Q E
V U D S X L Z E O K H I E Z M O N F A
C G S L R G L P X X A V S E G O Q E T
T L Q T W E M O B T I V T V Q D G M H
F G E Q A O C N I T I S Y E S A F A E
E P M A C I I Y C L Y N L G W P O C R
R B N P N M N A C S J A C E P E R I C
T O W W A A O A O L R L S T O S E D Z
I J R N I I I C B T I L B A P T S R E
L E U G D N E R U L S N R R U I T A N
I S L A A N D E A C E A G I L C D I D
T M R N R N N F G C A T D A A I F N A
Y A W Q I N I O A C T U A N T D G C N
B X L A O N X C U R D R N C I E M H G
B A M B O O O V F M M A N P O D F W E
E A R T H F R I E N D L Y Z N B S N R
M A S S T R A N S I T V R E C Y C L E
C G V M N D K F E A R T H D A Y T P D
```

5

			7			1	4	5
						3		
8				6				
	5		6					
	9	3	8	5				
				3	1			
		4	3		2			7
		6		1				
2				4		8		

SUDOKU 2 - EASY

7	4							
					1			
		2			9		4	8
	5				4			
					7	5	2	
2		3						1
1			9			8		
		6		8		7	9	
	2				3		5	

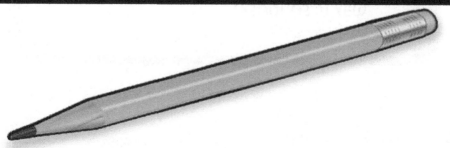

	N	O	O	T	I	A	Y	G	E	V	E	R	Y
		I	T	O	H	L	I	I	D	I	E		
		P	B	P	D	I	S		B	O	Y		
		N	M	U	T	N	G		S	L	S		
			E	H	O	S	E			A			
				P		N							

FALLEN QUOTES 2, 3

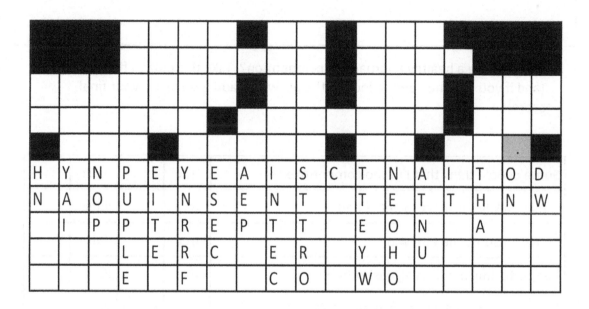

HOW COMPETITIVE ARE YOU?

Do you have a healthy approach to competition? Take this quiz to find out! (and if you feel the need to look at the answers...add 2 points to your final score)!

Some people think that I'm too competitive	true		false	
It takes a killer instinct to get ahead	true		false	
I have let someone else win	true		false	
I enjoy testing my skills against others	true		false	
I am at my best when competing with others	true		false	
I often try to beat the car next to me after a red light	true		false	
I turn almost everything into a contest	true		false	
I will be upset if I don't do well on this quiz	true		false	
I use a to-do list almost every day	true		false	
I have well defined goals	true		false	
I feel the need to be better than my siblings	true		false	
I am constantly learning new things	true		false	
I am a workaholic	true		false	
Score 1 point for each true answer. TOTAL =				

WHAT DOES YOUR SCORE MEAN?

0-4...You're actually anti-competitive. You are avoiding competitive situations which might mean you need a little more self-confidence. Some competition is a powerful motivator that helps you get ahead and contribute more.

5-8...You have a healthy level of competition. Keep up the good work!

9-13...You're going to be mad, but sorry, you didn't win this quiz! There's no denying your competitive nature and desire to succeed is a commendable quality, but stopping at nothing to come out on top can also become a problem when your competitiveness becomes all-consuming or takes the enjoyment away from others. Try to relax a little more!

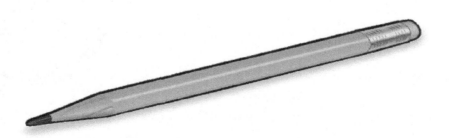

CROSSWORD 2

Across

2 Contract negotiator: Abbr.
3 The Trojans of the N.C.A.A.
5 Gut reaction?
9 Guarded
10 "It doesn't matter"
12 "For shame!"
14 "Concentration" pronoun
15 "Uh-uh!" (3,4,2,6)
20 Hooters (4,4)
21 Most recent
22 "To ___ is human ..."
23 "No way!" (3,1,6)
24 Not your
25 "Help!"
27 Narc's org.
29 Steady
32 ___-Magnon
33 Officer's query to a speeder (6,3,4)
37 Final: Abbr.
38 Funny business
42 By and by
45 Do some roadwork
46 Maxima maker
47 Actress Winger

(numbers at the end of clues indicate multiple word answer and their letter count)

Down

1 Elated (7,4)
2 "Aladdin" monkey
3 "Yoo-hoo!" (2,4)
4 Loc. ___
6 "Feels Like the First Time" band
7 Lots (5,1,3)
8 Fast one (5,5)
11 Book before Daniel: Abbr.
13 Meteorological phenomenon (6,9)
16 Releases
17 Bartender? (4,5)
18 Burlap fiber
19 Meeting place
26 "Beat it!"
27 "How obvious!"
28 Balloon filler
30 Substantial
31 Whimper
33 "Do ___ Diddy Diddy" (1964 hit)
34 Dusk, to Donne
35 Seat of White Pine County, Nev.
36 Computer file suffix
39 "___ in Calico" (1946 song)
40 Hate group
41 "Ol' Man River" composer
43 Felt bad about
44 "___ lost!"

plane section
pole
prime
product
QED
radians
ratio
residue
root
rule
scalar
scalene
separable
series
sign
smooth
space
sphere
subset
sum
tensor
variable
variance
vector
zero

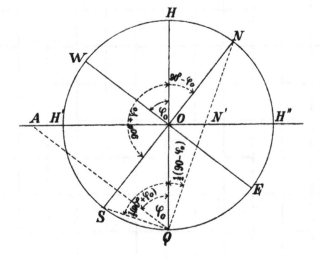

```
Y E L R O T C E V R M S V B J
K L R O Y F M E C U M A U Q H
O B X O R I S B S O R P Y K T
I A S T R E B P O I L P W Z M
T R C P P C Z T A A D E T B S
A A A O I V H B T C N M F N I
R P L G L F L E B E E H A L T
L E A Q O E S R L W P I Q E D
K S R P T E M A X U D O A Y E
K T I Z C H C M X A R H R T T
U W B T U S T C R R O S N E T
N G I S D W Y N E R E H P S D
Q O R F O R E S I D U E M B Q
N Y S E R I E S C R O X P U L
X X Z C P V A R I A N C E S M
```

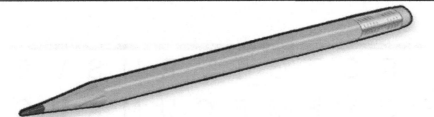

	9		7		4	1	6	
	3			1	2			
1					6		9	3
3		7	8					6
				4				9
				6	5		1	
			6	2	9	7	5	8
5	8	9				6		4
	2							1

SUDOKU 4 - EASY

	5						2	
9			1			6		
6			2	8	3			
2		5	3					
7		6		1	2			
			7	4			9	
5		7	9	6		8		3
						1		6
1	6		4		7	2		

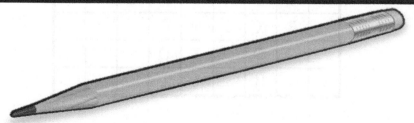

FALLEN QUOTES 4, 5

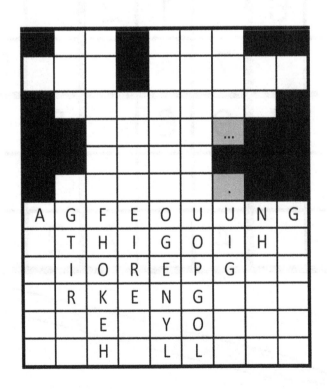

FALLEN QUOTES 6

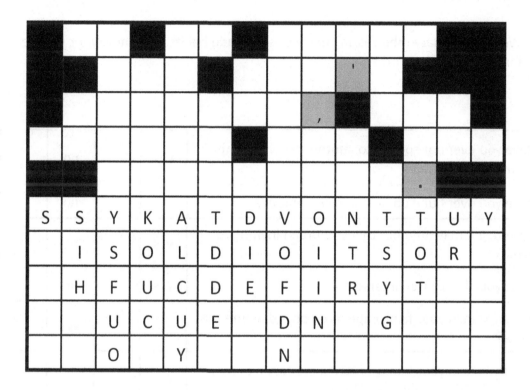

Random Thoughts...

When everything is coming your way, you're in the wrong lane.

HOW DYSFUNCTIONAL IS YOUR FAMILY?

We all have that embarrassing uncle or some odd habits. See how your unique family compares to others!

Have you ever not spoken to another family member for months at a time?	yes		no	
Have you ever hung up on a family member?	yes		no	
Is there a family member that you dread inviting to events?	yes		no	
Does your family tree intersect ?	yes		no	
Has anyone in your family appeared on a daytime talk show?	yes		no	
Has anyone in your family gotten a restraining order against another family member?	yes		no	
Has someone in your family embarrassed you?	yes		no	
Is there regular yelling in your household?	yes		no	
When you compare family craziness with friends do you usually win?	yes		no	
Has anyone in your family run away from home?	yes		no	
Does your family gossip about each other?	yes		no	
Is your family very large or very small?	yes		no	
Score 1 point for each yes answer. TOTAL =				

WHAT DOES YOUR SCORE MEAN?

0-4 Seriously, your family is a little boring. But perfectly healthy and balanced. You should seriously consider marrying someone with a little more dysfunction just to keep things interesting.

5-8 Congratulations! Like most families yours is a little quirky and dysfunctional. Life would be a lttle boring otherwise.

9-16 Wow...your family is seriously dysfunctional. I hope someone will make some money on that book.

PRESIDENTIAL TRIVIA CROSSWORD 3

Across

3 Had a dog named Veto
5 Refused to use the telephone
8 Loved jelly beans
10 Was a fashion model
11 First president born in a log cabin
12 Acquired California during his term
13 Held the first Inaugural Ball
15 Only president born in California
18 In charge of D-Day invasion
19 Gave the White House its name
20 1st to name an African American to his cabinet
21 Succeeded Garfield upon his assassination
22 First President to be a Rhodes Scholar

Down

1 The only president from Indiana
2 Was a successful tailer
4 Once captured by pirates
6 First President spelunker
7 First President to wear pants
9 First to put a Christmas tree in the White House
11 Attended seances at the White House
12 The only bachelor President
14 On the $50
16 Great-great-great nephew of John Tyler
17 Had 15 children

23

Adriatic
Aral Sea
Atlantic
Baikal
Baltic
Bass Sea
Black Sea
Caribbean
Chukotsk Sea
Cook Strait
Coral Sea
East China Sea
Flores Sea
Gulf of Oman
Hudson Bay
Irish Sea
Kara Sea
Lake Chad
Lake Erie
Lake Maracaibo
Loch Ness
North Sea
Pacific
Red Sea
Skaggerak
South China Sea
Strait of Malacca
Timor Sea
White Sea
Yellow Sea

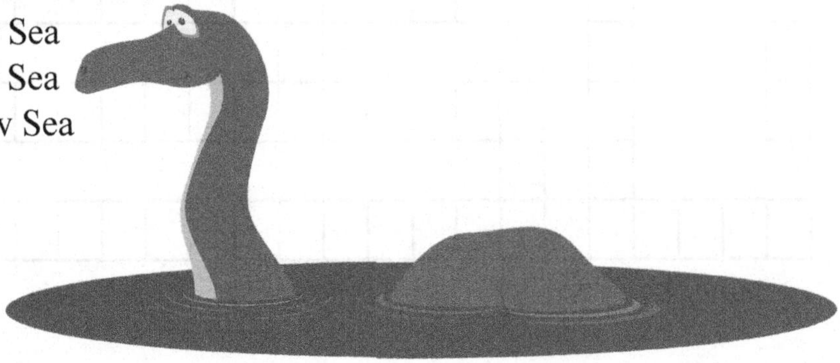

```
C H U K O T S K S E A L P C G Z E
S A E M A T C Z K E B A I K A L J
T E N O E I J O S G C T D J H N B
R S Y L S M G D R I N S B A P A R
A E X O S O E U F A D T D C L E A
I T V B E R U I L L L A Q T K B E
T I C I R S C T A F E S I Q A B S
O H I A O E A K H S O C E X R I H
F W T C L A E Z S C C F I A E R T
M A A A F C S S E N H C O L G A R
A H I R H L A K E E R I E M G C O
L L R A T B K H U D S O N B A Y N
A V D M A E S L A R A V M A K N K
C K A E I A E S A N I H C T S A E
C O O K S T R A I T I S T R G E P
A B L A C K S E A I R I S H S E A
Y E L L O W S E A H K A R A S E A
```

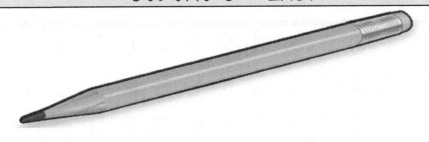

	8		9			5	7	
2						1		
				3	4			
		3				2	9	
						4		
	9	2	7	6				
	1		4					9
						7		
			2	7	3		8	

SUDOKU 6 - EASY

		4			2			6
				1				7
6		1	7	3				
			6					
7				2	8			
	8			7			9	3
	2			5				8
5			1	8	9		7	

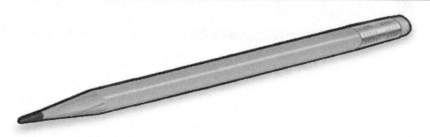

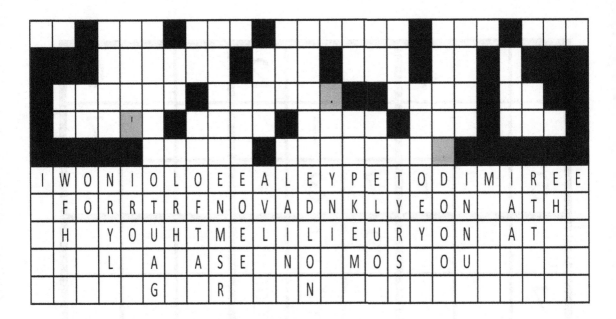

Random Thoughts...

If your dog is fat, you aren't getting enough exercise.

FALLEN QUOTES - 8, 9

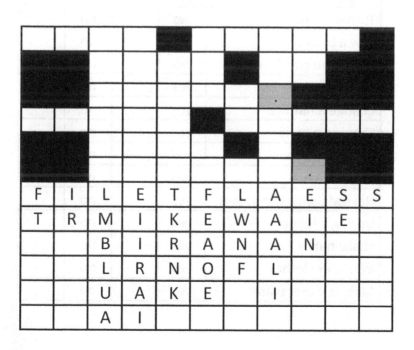

50 THINGS EVERY MAN SHOULD KNOW HOW TO DO !

Okay, this list is a bit sexist, but men are still judged on how capable they are in many different areas. See how many you have mastered!

Tie a necktie	yes		no	
Build a campfire	yes		no	
Shine your shoes	yes		no	
Change a car fuse	yes		no	
Parallel park	yes		no	
Paddle a canoe	yes		no	
Fix a leaky faucet	yes		no	
Treat a burn	yes		no	
Grill with charcoal	yes		no	
Set up a tent	yes		no	
Throw a baseball	yes		no	
Throw a football	yes		no	
Throw a Frisbee	yes		no	
Sew a button	yes		no	
Make one good dinner	yes		no	
Split firewood	yes		no	
Change a flat tire	yes		no	
Sharpen a knife	yes		no	
Change a diaper	yes		no	
Give a speech	yes		no	
Navigate with a compass	yes		no	
Unclog a toilet	yes		no	
Shake hands	yes		no	
Iron your clothes	yes		no	
Make a paper plane	yes		no	

Shuffle cards	yes		no	
Play poker	yes		no	
Throw a punch	yes		no	
Do a perfect push up	yes		no	
Cook a steak	yes		no	
Change a cars oil	yes		no	
Whistle	yes		no	
Tie a hook on a fishing line	yes		no	
Jump start a car	yes		no	
Slow dance	yes		no	
Tie a tourniquet	yes		no	
The Heimlich maneuver	yes		no	
Fillet a fish	yes		no	
Hang a picture	yes		no	
Open a beer without an opener	yes		no	
Tell at least one good joke	yes		no	
Calculate square footage	yes		no	
Hammer a nail (well)	yes		no	
Give a speech	yes		no	
Make a bed	yes		no	
Play pool	yes		no	
Dress a wound	yes		no	
Play blackjack	yes		no	
Negotiate a better price	yes		no	
Score 1 point for each yes answer on both pages TOTAL =				

WHAT DOES YOUR SCORE MEAN?

0-15...Good start, but it's time to get out there and gain some life skills!

16-30...You're doing fine. Try to add a few more skills to your repertoire.

31-50...Congratulations! You can hold your own in many situations.

CROSSWORD 4

Across

3 "Scream" director Craven
6 Italian, e.g.
8 Rattles
11 Control
12 Discounted (2,4)
15 Be itinerant
16 Blah-blah-blah
17 His "4" was retired
18 "Thank You (Falettinme Be Mice ___ Again)" (#1 hit of 1970)
19 "And ___ bed"
21 Catch, in a way
23 Place to find keys (10,5)
25 Often memorized math term
27 Outer: Prefix
29 End of the question
30 Foolish
32 X's
33 "Keystone Kops" producer
34 Dear
35 Carve in stone
36 "___ the fields we go"
37 Phrase on the back of a buck (2,3,2,5)
38 Buttonwood
41 "Yes ___?" (2,2)
42 "That was a close one!"
43 Bout stopper, for short
44 "Duino Elegies" poet
45 Anemic (5-7)

(numbers at the end of clues indicate multiple word answer and their letter count)

Down

1 "Bravo!" (4,3)
2 End of the quote (5,6)
3 Ring org.
4 "Enough already!"
5 Response to "grazie"
6 Check mate?
7 No matter what (4,4,2,5)
9 Hack
10 Pan-fries
13 Cover letters?
14 Go ballistic (4,4,4)
20 Buckle (5,2,3,5)
22 "... ___ quit!"
24 Fails (4,2,3)
25 Dazed and confused
26 Head honcho (3,6)
28 Eager (5-6)
31 Prefix with -phile
35 Recluse
39 Sagan of "Cosmos"
40 Density symbol
42 Loan figure: Abbr.

WORD FIND 4 - FAMOUS PEOPLE

Al Gore
Ann Rice
B. B. King
Bill Clinton
Bill Gates
Bob Dole
Bono
Cher
Elton John
Elvira
Eminem
Fergie
Gerald Ford
John Glenn
Kate Moss
Liberace
Mary Hart
Mia Hamm
Neil Young
P. Diddy
Pele
Prince
Rihanna
Seal
Selena
Shakira
Star Jones
Steffi Graf
Will Smith

```
A A J K A T E M O S S A H W C
N E I L Y O U N G J R E X Y H
S T A R J O N E S I C U A M E
N W B G O Q O E V V M L L L R
B I I E H M T L I B E R A C E
B L L R N A E A N N R I C E A
K L L A G F S H A K I R A N I
I S C L L B O B D O L E E J E
N M L D E J E B X D B L D L A
G I I F N F E R G I E O E N L
B T N O N B M H U S M P N D G
R H T R P R I N C E F A E O O
U L O D W T N M I A H A M M R
E C N T S T E F F I G R A F E
P D I D D Y M A R Y H A R T C
```

6		7			4			
1			2		8			
	5			1		6		
		5				4		
			4		2			3
						9	2	8
	2			4				
7			1		3			
4	8					1		

							9	2
4	8					3		
	9	5	7					
7	6		3	4			5	
1							6	
	3							
		8	2		9	6		
					3	9		
			6				8	4

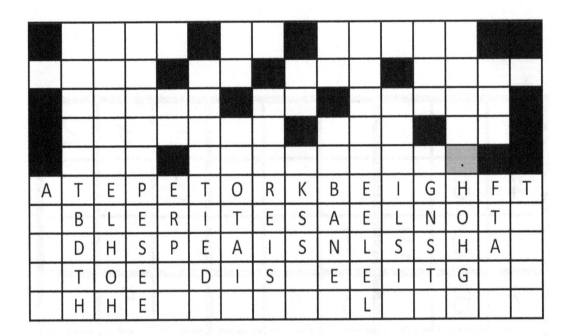

Random Thoughts...

Do Vegetarians eat animal crackers?

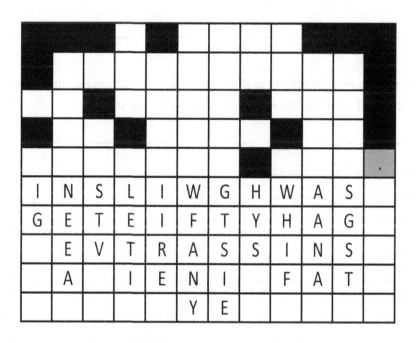

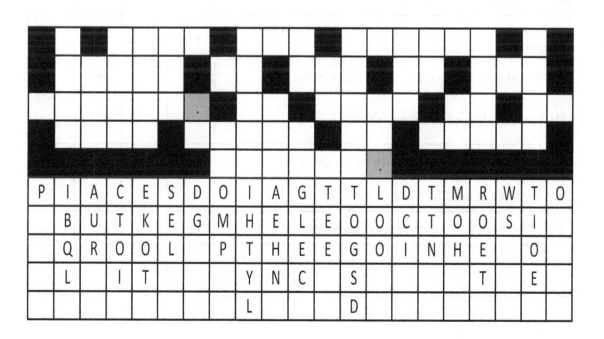

ARE YOU CHEAP ?

Being frugal is an admirable quality. But when it crosses the line into cheap... not so good. Take this test to see if you're a penny pincher!

Have you ever re-gifted a present?	yes		no	
Do you regularly shop at the Dollar Tree?	yes		no	
Have you ever been lectured for not leaving a big enough tip?	yes		no	
Do you clip coupons every week?	yes		no	
Do you compare prices on almost everything you buy?	yes		no	
Do you prefer to calculate everyones dinner portion instead of dividing it equally?	yes		no	
Do you pick up every penny you see laying on the ground?	yes		no	
Do you always order off of the value menu?	yes		no	
Do you buy discounted meat or milk?	yes		no	
Do you only buy clothes if they're on sale?	yes		no	
Have you ever bought a brand new car?	no		yes	
Do other people think that you're poor?	yes		no	
Score 1 point for each answer in the first column TOTAL =				

WHAT DOES YOUR SCORE MEAN ?

0-4...If you're not lacking for money, keep doing what you're doing. You're definitely not cheap. If you find that you're short sometimes, you should try some money saving ideas.

5-8...You love hunting down a great deal, but you're also willing to spend your money. You have a good handle on your money.

9-12... You are so concerned about saving money that you are getting obsessed. Loosen up and enjoy life a little!

CROSSWORD 5

Across

1 Live wire, so to speak
3 Clod chopper
7 Restraining order?
9 I.R.S. employee: Abbr.
11 Mint family member
13 Hangup
14 Trips
16 Dirty coat
17 Motor suffix, commercially
18 This puzzle's theme (3,5,5)
21 "Fancy that!"
22 French pronoun
24 Nonsense
26 Kids Racer (2-4)
27 Barely get, with "out"
28 Trophy
29 End of the quip
31 Baker's dozen?
32 Picture starring 11D/55D (5,4,6)
33 Boat propellers
35 A.C. letters
37 Functions
39 ___-Mart
40 Even if, briefly
41 "Idylls of the King" character
43 Abbr. on a French envelope
44 They hold tin cups
45 1960's radical grp.
46 Keystone character

(numbers at the end of clues indicate multiple word answer and their letter count)

Down

2 Biochemistry abbr.
3 Birthright
4 "Chicago" lyricist
5 Central Park sight
6 Shabby
7 Colorful language (4-6,5)
8 "___ Perpetua" (Idaho's motto)
10 Coup ___
12 Brit. record label
15 Hon (7-3)
16 Direct
19 Turn in (3,3,3)
20 Rage (5,4)
23 Set off
25 Goes postal (5,2)
30 Fix, as a pump
34 Gonorrhea, e.g.: Abbr.
35 Hard knocks
36 Admiral's org.
37 Fat unit
38 Armageddon
40 French possessive
42 AOL, e.g.
43 French title abbr.

WORD FiND 5 - FOOD

arrowroot
basket
Bath bun
beat
beer
besom
bread
can
carafe
chef
chianti
chuck
cloche
cob
crown
dish
eggs
escalope
flan
goose
gruyere
haunch of mutton
hot
ice box
match
mess
mixer
mug
mulled cider

pease
rare
reduce
roll
salad
shank
simnel
soup
soy
syrup
tea
tomato
trace
trap
trivet
tub
tuna
urn
vegetable cutter
waffle
yolk

```
T U N A I G R U Y E R E N N G A Q
E O G D S Z M H H U E F S V U R N
G N M Z K H W S C P D G Y E P R N
C H I A N T I E J L U B R G H O O
S O U P T D P E S X C E U E T W P
F N Z C Z O U G O X E E P T R R H
W A F F L E G B C Q P R U A I O O
C A R A F E E U A N E M C B V O T
N H C L O C H E N X F E O L E T Y
B S U R I A S L I O L S T E T O C
E E B C O S I M H L A S R C S M O
S H A N K W M C D P N E A U T U B
O S S T L P N A M Q S Y C T F G E
M A K N A U E Z T O J T E T N R Y
A L E R A R L A O C H E F E A K O
B A T H B U N G S H H A C R O L L
H D C R R M U L L E D C I D E R K
```

1	6			5				
	5	9			8			
				7				
			2		3			9
	2		7			5		8
	8				6		7	
	4				2		1	
						6	9	2
								7

2		6				4		
	8			9			1	
						7		
5			8		6		3	
7					9		4	
		2				1		
			6					3
				4			2	
			9	2	8	5		

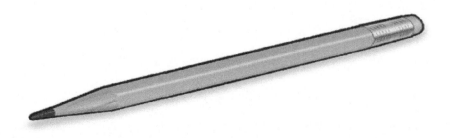

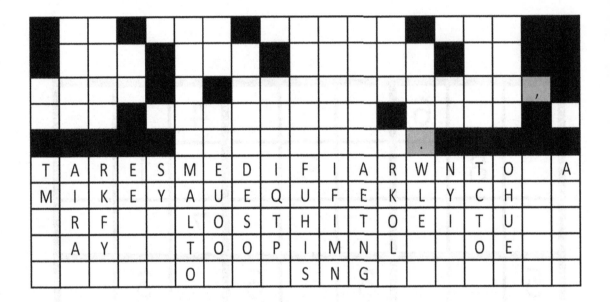

Random Thoughts...

A boiled egg is hard to beat.

FALLEN QUOTES - 14, 15

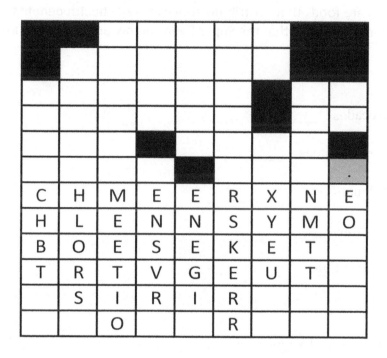

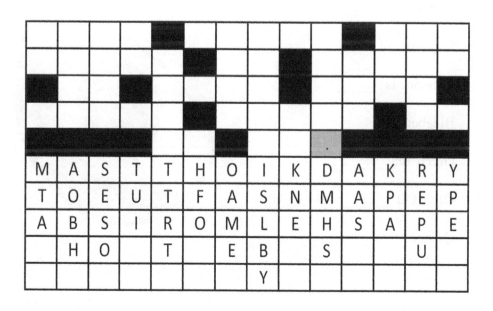

SUPER FOODS QUIZ

Super foods are foods that contribute above average health benefits. See if you can find the benefit that the Super Foods below are best know for.

Avocados _____

Sweet Potatoes _____

Walnuts _____

Kim Chi _____

Organic Eggs _____

Kale _____

Unsweetened Yogurt _____

Salmon _____

Turmeric _____

Coconut Oil _____

Chia Seeds _____

Blueberries _____

Green Tea _____

Olive Oil _____

Quinoa _____

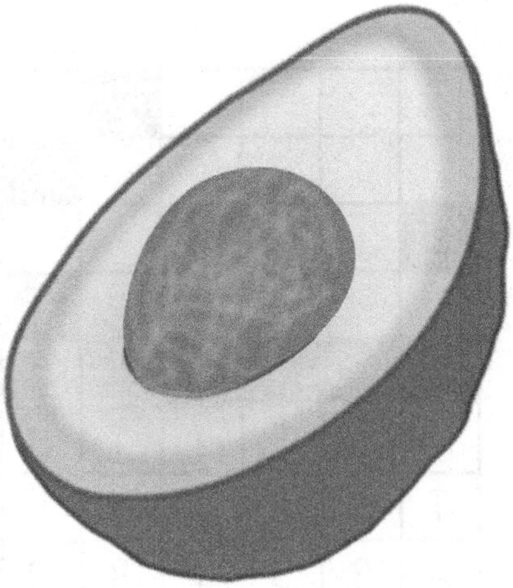

A. Great for your brain, memory and packed with healthy fat and fiber. Great in salads and cookies.

B. A gluten free supergrain higher in protein and fiber than most other grains.

C. Boosts the immune system and contains probiotics.

D. Source of fat that increases good cholesterol. Might actually help with burning fat.

E. Excellent source of antioxidants, boosts focus and memory and linked to helping prevent skin cancer. Also, they're really good in muffins.

F. Full of healthy monounsaturated fats and linked to a healthy heart. Sensitive to light and high heat.

G. Tiny whole grain that's full of omega-3 fatty acids, fiber, antioxidants and minerals. Can be used as a thickener.

H. Contains probiotic that aids in digestion. Traditional Korean food.

I. Orange color indicative of its excellent source of Vitamin A, beta-carotene and fiber.

J. Super anti-cancer properties, especially against prostate cancer.

K. Contains a high level of healthy Omega-3 fatty acids that reduces inflammation. Best if sourced from the wild instead of farmed.

L. Packed with antioxidants and anti-inflammatory properties, this food is also nonfat and full of vitamins. Common in Indian cuisine.

M. Contains healthy unsaturated fat and fiber and more potassium than bananas. They are technically a fruit and will ripen quicker with an apple nearby.

N. Low in calories, high in fiber, zero fat, packed with Vitamin A, C and K and antioxidants. Bake and salt for a healthy replacement for chips.

O. Full of protein, B-Vitamins, choline, lutein and often called the perfect food.

Avocados...M, Sweet Potatoes...I, Walnuts ...A, Kim Chi...H, Organic Eggs ...O, Kale...N, Unsweetened Yogurt...C, Salmon...K, Turmeric...L, Coconut Oil...D, Chia Seeds...G, Blueberries...E, Green Tea...J, Olive Oil...F, Quinoa...B.

CROSSWORD 6

Across

1 Feelers
4 Boeing 747, e.g.
6 "How's tricks?" (5,3)
10 Dry riverbed
12 Popular cocktail (7,4)
16 Cracker Jack bonus
17 Former Serbian capital
19 1814 Byron poem
20 High ground (3,8,4)
22 Quite some time (1,5,2,7)
24 Cheap
25 Shrink
26 The "p" in m.p.g.
27 Nonstop (3,2,3,3,3)
30 Angry
32 Kind of network
35 About (2,2)
37 Develop
40 Ecstasy
42 Italian for "to the tooth" (2,5)
44 Parade
45 Disoriented
49 Do followers
51 Carpentry tool
52 One of the Kennedys
53 Invoice abbr.
54 See circled squares

(numbers at the end of clues indicate multiple word answer and their letter count)

Down

1 Freely (2,4)
2 Rx instruction
3 Book after Galatians: Abbr.
4 Madison or Monroe: Abbr.
5 Athletic supporter?
6 Tony and Maria Musical (4,4,5)
7 Prefix with pressure
8 Unappealing (3,4,3,2,3)
9 Explanations
11 Because (2,2,4,2)
13 Better (7,2)
14 "Rock and Roll, Hoochie ___" (1974 hit)
15 Puts back on eBay
18 Loud
21 Kind of race
23 Reputation ruiner (10,5)
25 Engine sound
28 "Aladdin" monkey
29 Mrs. Addams, to Gomez
31 Dressed (up)
33 Brontë's "Jane ___"
34 Lift (4,3)
36 Expels
37 Veteran
38 "___ cost to you!" (2,2)
39 Nutty confection
41 Expunges
43 Chinese "way"
46 "The wolf ___ the door"
47 Math class, for short
48 ...
49 "In the Good Old Summertime" lyricist Shields
50 Medical suffix

WORD FIND 6 - JOBS

Accountant
Architect
Artist
Baker
Buyer
Care assistant
Caretaker
Carpenter
Cashier
Chef
Chemist
Civil servant
Cleaner
Clerk
Cook
Counsellor
Courier
Doctor
Driver
Editor
Engineer
Farmer
IT manager
Lawyer

Lecturer
Librarian
Mechanic
Musician
Nanny
Nurse
Physicist
Pilot
Plumber
Printer
Production manager
Surgeon
Teacher
Trainer
Turner
Tutor
Typist
Waiter
Waitress
Welder

```
W A I T R E S S G V F R R U T T F H C
A L A W Y E R E K A T E R A C N E D A
I R T S I T R A R R Y I S C E A H X E
T C N E C N D M A U Z R U C T V C P X
E N I Z F O E I B B E U R O I R S R R
R C N N C R N P R K Q O G U H E R E E
I H T T A E F E A V N C E N C S E T R
U C O N R H V B Z P I A O T R L T N U
I R L M A I C W Z C E L N A A I N E T
T H I E R T R E N A E L C N J V I P C
M P B D R T S I M E H C B T Y I R R E
A W R A X K O I T R E I H S A C P A L
N N A M A D R F S Y T E A C H E R C L
A U R E D L E W G S P H Y S I C I S T
G R I P H K N X Y N A I C I S U M R P
E S A U Y O R R O L L E S N U O C O I
R E N S E O U E D I T O R T V N E T L
P R O D U C T I O N M A N A G E R U O
E N G I N E E R E B M U L P C H W T T
```

SUDOKU 11 - MEDIUM

		5			1	4	3	
					9			8
		7	2				1	
			3	9				2
		9				8		
1				5	7			
	6				8	2		
5			1					
	7	8	6			3		

SUDOKU 12 - MEDIUM

7	9							2
6			7		2			9
	3							
					8		2	1
					6	3		
			9	1			8	7
		1	8		4			
				3				
		5					9	8

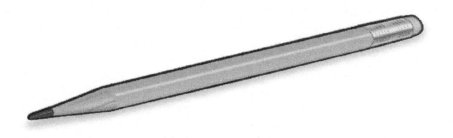

57

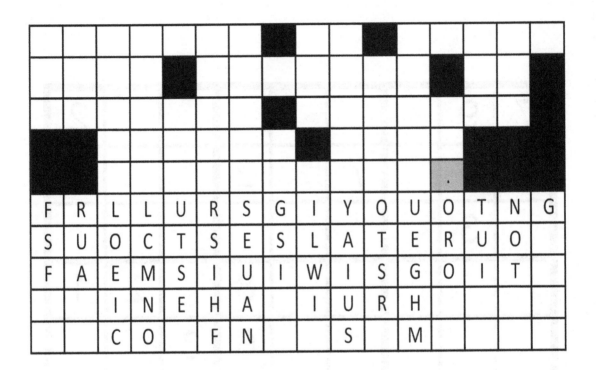

Dumb Joke...

What's the difference between snowmen and snowwomen?

(answer on page 110)

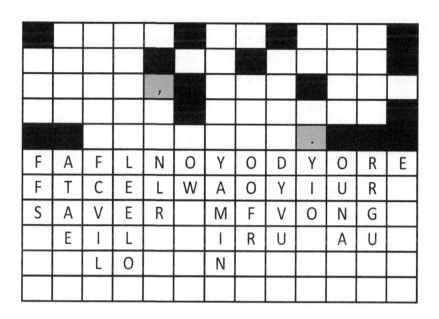

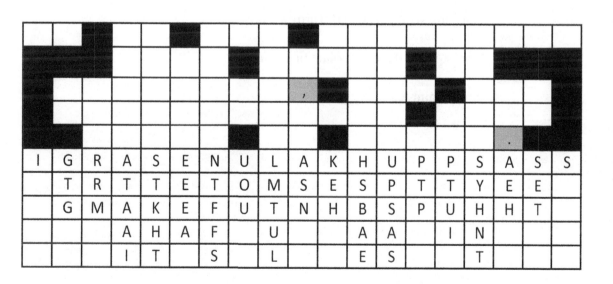

NATURAL REMEDIES

Below are some surprisingly effective and inexpensive home remedies. See if you can match them with what they are proven to help treat.
(this test is just for fun - please check with your doctor before trying to use anything to treat your symptoms)!

Ginger _____

Linden Flower Tea _____

Oatmeal _____

Tea with lemon and honey _____

Two teaspoons of sugar _____

Cherries _____

Aloe Vera _____

Gargling with garlic and warm water _____

Two squares dark chocolate or honey _____

Peppermint tea _____

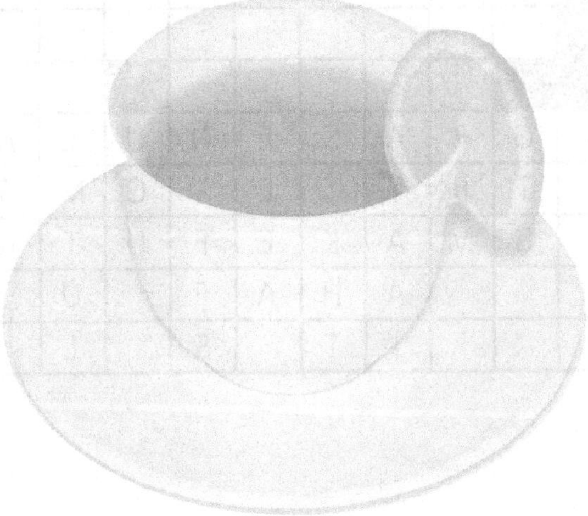

A.   Can reduce the length of a cold

B.   Curbs a cough

C.   Sooths a burn

D.   Quells nausea

E.   Stops hiccups

F.   Soothes sore throats and wards off vampires

G.   Helps you sleep

H.   Reduces fever

I.   Prevents farting...or at least makes them smell a little better

J.   Steeped in water will help relieve dry itchy skin

Ginger...D, Linden Flower Tea...H, Oatmeal ..J, Tea with lemon and honey...B, Two teaspoons
of sugar ...E, Cherries...G, Aloe Vera...C, Garling with garlic and warm water...F,
Two squares of dark chocolate or honey...A, Peppermint Tea...L
Blueberries...E, Green Tea...J, Olive Oil...F, Quinoa...B.

CROSSWORD 7

Across

1 Garden decorations
4 Mercedes competitor
6 Bluecoat
9 Butt
11 Retreats
14 Red state
16 Part of E.E.C.: Abbr.
18 "Beats me" (1,6,3,1,4)
21 Long Island town
22 Danger signal
23 Sailing ropes
24 P.I., e.g.
25 Trunk item (3,6)
27 Surrounding glows
28 ___ cry
29 Proportionately (3,4)
30 The "S" in R.S.V.P.
31 A abroad
32 Ancient
33 Destroy
34 Awakens (5,2)
36 Head honcho (3,9)
38 Full of vigor
40 ___-Locka, Fla.
41 Combination punch?
43 Airs
45 Acrylic fiber
46 Fuddy-duddy (3-9)

Down

2 Masefield play "The Tragedy of ___ "
3 Yemen, once
5 Heads overseas?
6 Creamy desserts with ladyfingers (9,6)
7 "Easy!" (5,2,4)
8 California's ___ Valley
10 Crumble (2,2,6)
12 Hard to grasp (8,2,2,3)
13 Suffix with sermon (0-3)
15 Boris Godunov, for one
17 Fast (9,6)
19 Kilmer of "At First Sight"
20 This puzzle's theme (3,5,5)
22 "Wow!"
26 Danish cheese
28 Fast one
29 Brownish purple
34 Pandemonium
35 Jazz trombonist Kid ___
37 Comedians real name was Arthur
39 Bit of color
41 Scooby-___ (cartoon dog)
42 Gonorrhea, e.g.: Abbr.
44 Altar avowal

(numbers at the end of clues indicate multiple word answer and their letter count)

62

WORD FIND 7 - MUSICAL INSTRUMENTS

accordion
anvil
banjo
bellharp
bin
bones
bugelhorn
bugle
cello
cheng
chimes
citar
clarinet
crwth
cymbal
ditalharp
dulcimer
electronic piano
fife
flute
gong
guitar
hand bell
hurdygurdy
klavier
lyre
mandolin
marina
melotron
moog
oboe

organ
pipe
quail
rattle
rebec
shawm
snare drum
stock horn
tabor
tambour
timpani
tromba
tuba
vina
viola
violin
virginal
zimbalon
zither

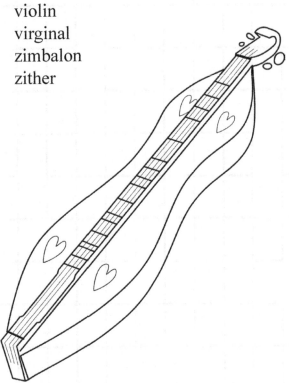

```
Q P X E R K V F C N E C C T B O N E S
T T O Z L R W R I H L I G U I T A R K
I R B I K X E B Q M E A N V I L A H M
M O O M G I Z N H W C N O T K T M X N
P M E B V Z I I U A T Z G Z I N Z I W
A B A A A U T L R H R A V C Q R L Y R
N A L L S T H O D S O N M B B O V V U
I K S O O O E I Y L N I A A D H D R O
D V R N S I R V G C I R R N N K U E B
P I A B U T V B U L C A A J O C S M M
C R T T N Z U D R A P M U O I O N I A
R G T A C G R E D R I Z E Q D T A C T
W I L Q L Y R E Y I A W C L R S R L F
T N E E H M K B N N N H E O M E U I
H A B V O P A B P E O A I Y C T D D F
R L R L K X I R A T C G M V C E R L E
B E L L H A R P P L Q R E O A X U O M
T E L L E B D N A H J O S M O T M T N
C I P I A Z M H K N R O H L E G U B D
```

9		7			5			
	8	2			3	4	7	
					8			2
	3		6	9			8	
4			8			2		
	2							
			5			9		
1	5			7			6	
		4						

				3	8			6
4							3	
			4	2			9	
	5	8						
	4			9				1
		1			3			5
		6						7
	2						6	
	9		6			1	8	

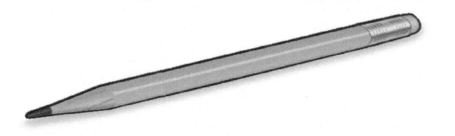

67

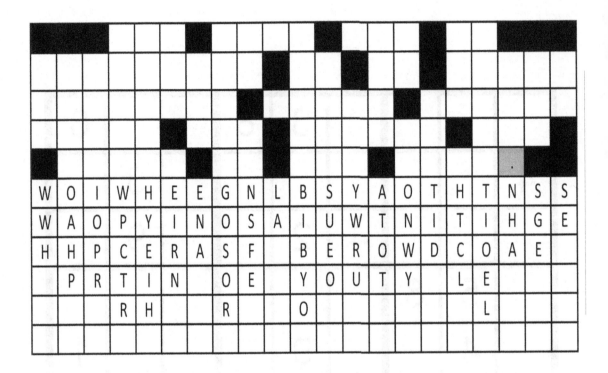

W	O	I	W	H	E	E	G	N	L	B	S	Y	A	O	T	H	T	N	S	S
W	A	O	P	Y	I	N	O	S	A	I	U	W	T	N	I	T	I	H	G	E
H	H	P	C	E	R	A	S	F		B	E	R	O	W	D	C	O	A	E	
	P	R	T	I	N		O	E		Y	O	U	T	Y		L	E	L		
		R	H			R				O							L			

Dumb Joke...

What do you call a bear with no teeth?

(answer on page 110)

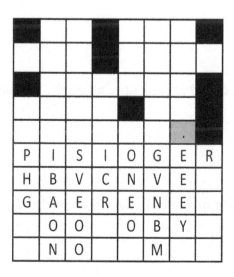

MENS FACTS AND HEALTH QUIZ

Take the quiz below to see how well you know random facts about the health and wellness of your fellow man...

1) What is the height of the average US man?
   a) 5 feet 7 inches
   b) 5 feet 8 inches
   c) 5 feet 9 inches
   d) 5 feet 10 inches

2) By age 50, what percent of men have male pattern baldness?
   a) 20%
   b) 30%
   c) 40%
   d) 50%

3) Boys represent what percentage of children in special education?
   a) 35%
   b) 50%
   c) 60%
   d) 75%

4) What percent of US men are circumcised?
   a) 36%
   b) 43%
   c) 56%
   d) 78%

5) Men represent what percent of all on the job fatalities
   a) 50%
   b) 65%
   c) 82%
   d) 94%

6) What percent of nurses in the US are male?
   a) 5%
   b) 20%
   c) 40%

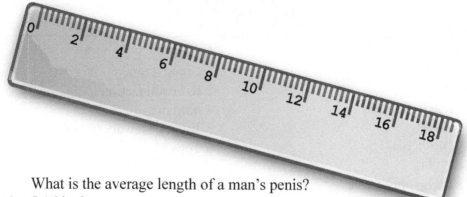

7)   What is the average length of a man's penis?
   a)   5.16 inches
   b)   5.58 inches
   c)   6.12 inches
   d)   6.51 inches

8)   Men are how many times more likely to commit murder than women?
   a)   2x
   b)   5x
   c)   10x

9)   What is the leading cause of death in males 15-24?
   a)   Suicide
   b)   Heart disease
   c)   Car accidents

10)   Men can produce milk from their breasts
   a)   True
   b)   False

11)   Men's faces age better than a woman's
   a)   True
   b)   False

12)   Men are more likely to suffer from depression than women
   a)   True
   b)   False

1...c, 2...d, 3...d, 4...c, 5...d, 6...a, 7...a, 8...c, 9...c, 10...a, 11...a, 12...b

CROSSWORD 8

Across

1 Chicken
3 Abase
6 French pronoun
9 Drawing
13 Dirty coat
14 Living
17 Ascap alternative
18 Neighbor of Tenn.
20 Repeating
21 Stink
22 Hearst's captors: Abbr.
24 Blouse, e.g.
26 Some are vital
27 Curt
29 "Lord, is ___?"
30 Big inits. in trucks
31 Head, slangily
32 Scale notes
33 Loc. ___
34 Milk: Prefix
36 City on the Susquehanna
37 Bird ___
38 "___ Doone" (1869 novel)
40 Cooler
41 Nonconformists
42 "La la" preceder
43 Boom producer
47 Inner: Prefix
48 Desire (5,3)
49 "How ___ Has the Banshee Cried"
(Thomas Moore poem) (7,8)

Down

1 China's Sun ___-sen
2 K-O connection
4 not your
5 Jimmy Stewart syllables
6 Tops (3,4)
7 Direct (2,3,5)
8 Part of BYO
10 Here, elsewhere
11 Quits (5,2,3,5)
12 Goodwill, e.g. (10,5)
15 "Rocky ___"
16 International understanding (7,8)
17 flock with each other (5,2,1,7)
19 Sue Grafton's "___ for Alibi"
23 "___ Olvidados" (1950 Luis
Buñuel film)
25 Relish
28 Carefree
30 Magnanimousness
35 Join, redundantly (5,2)
39 QB protectors
44 L.B.J.'s successor
45 Tokyo, formerly
46 Buffalo's summer hrs.

(numbers at the end of clues indicate multiple word answer and their letter count)

WORD FIND 8 - RELIGION

Adam
Anglican
Calvinistical
cardinal
clean
cosher
damned
Daniel
deadly
dean
doomed
errancy
Esau
Esther
Eve
gradual
Hallel
Haman
Hell
impure
Inferno
Jacob
Jonah
Joseph
Last Day

laver
limbo
Lot
Magi
manna
minor
missal
mortal
nonkosher
nuncio
parable
pax
Rota
Russian Orthodox
Seder
shibah
shiva
Sodom
tref
venial

```
Y D C N E I G A M Z X X E Y E J D
N A J W A L R B P A X O L S O T P
I M D L L E A E C A R D I N A L S
M N E T H I D R D E A O A O N U H
P E M S S N U R V E V H X N G B I
U D O L X A A A D T S T D K L O B
R C O I A D L N G O L R G O I C A
E R D M M T P C M L A O X S C A H
C V A B C O O Y I E I N H H A J F
M D J O I W R R S E N A P E N E E
A I C I N J H T S F E I E R R N L
N O N L F W H A A Q V S S T D A B
N S H O E E U V L L C S O D O M A
A N J P R A O S Q L G U J C R A R
E D G W N U N C I O E R W I R H A
V V V X O L S H I V A L H E L L P
F O E D L A C I T S I N I V L A C
```

			3		7			
		9	4				8	
			8		1	9		
		3	2			1		
		2				3		
	8		1		3	7		
	3		5	4				
6		4		1				
	7				8			6

SUDOKU 16 - MEDIUM

				4	7	2		
7			2		9			
	9				3	1	4	
		9						
			5				8	
	1	3		7				
		5				3		8
1								
	7		1	2				9

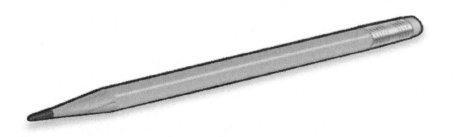

P	H	E	A	M	T	B	N	O	T	F	O	R	O	F	H	R	R
L	H	E	N	R	T	I	L	T	I	C	G	E	Q	T	F	M	Y
	T	E	I		S	E		U	L		I	N	B	N	G	U	E	E
	A	T						I	O			O					O
						T	T										

Dumb Joke...

How do you buy four suits for a dollar?

(answer on page 110)

FALLEN QUOTES 23, 24

SUPER HERO TRIVIA

Take the quiz below to see how well you know your Super Heroes !

1.   Which Avenger can communicate with birds? _____

2.   Lex Luther is the enemy of which Superhero? _____

3.   Aunt May is the guardian of which Superhero? _____

4.   This Superhero gets his power from a ring _____

5.   Which X-Man did actor Hugh Jackman play? _____

6.   Which Superheros got their powers while they were astronauts? _____

7.   Who was working as a Police Scientist when they got their powers? _____

8.   What is the favorite food of the TMNT's? _____

9.   Who is also known as the Caped Crusader? _____

10.   Who is Superman's cousin? _____

11.   Bruce Banner becomes which Superhero? _____

12.   Which Superhero owns Area 51? _____

13.   Asgard is the home planet of which Superhero? _____

14.   Vibranium Steel was used to make this Superhero's defense. _____

15.   Which Superhero's home is Paradise Island? _____

a. Thor

b. Pizza

c. Superman

d. Wolverine

e. The Flash

f. Falcon

g. Pizza

h. Wonder Woman

i. Supergirl

j. Spiderman

k. Iron Man

l. Green Lantern

m. Captain America

n. The Fantastic Four

o. Wonder Woman

p. Batman

q. The Hulk

1...f, 2...c, 3...j, 4...l, 5...d, 6...n, 7...e, 8...b, 9...p, 10...i, 11...q, 12...k, 13...a, 14...m, 15...h

CROSSWORD 9

Across

1 Not coming after down (9,2)
6 Dash
8 Colorful language (4-6,5)
11 "Be quiet!"
12 Unified
13 Dadaism founder
15 Allergic reaction
17 Big ___ Conference
18 Certain Scandinavian
20 Embraces
21 Blah-blah-blah
22 Boob tubes
23 Devours (8,3)
28 Binge
30 Sonora shawls
32 Help for checkers
33 Chiang ___-shek
34 Dude
36 BBQ annoyance
38 Chip off the old block
40 1956 Elvis song (10,5)

Down

1 Marching band instruments
2 End of the query
3 Jerk
4 Score
5 Revolts
6 Detachable container
7 3.1415
9 Render unnecessary
10 Green light (5,2,8)
14 El ___, Tex.
16 Hack
17 Puts two and two together? (5,2)
19 Suffix with president
24 Small carriage (3-6)
25 Bits
26 Lodge
27 Pool opening
29 Clear
31 Atl. crosser
35 "Stupid me!"
36 Little, in Leith
37 Biochemistry abbr.
39 "Flying Down to ___"

(numbers at the end of clues indicate multiple word answer and their letter count)

WORD FIND 9 - BRANDS

Band Aid
bennie
Carboloy
Clorox
Colt
Duralumin
Gortex
Hoover
Invar
Kleenex
Lilo
Loafer
Lucite
Luger
Maalox
Magic Marker
Masonite
Meccano
Mylanta
Orlon
Xerox
Perspex
Pyrex
Rolaids
Scotch tape
Scrabble
Silex
Sno-cat
Spam
Stellite
Styrofoam
Teflon
Thermos
Tums
Velcro
Viyella
Xerox

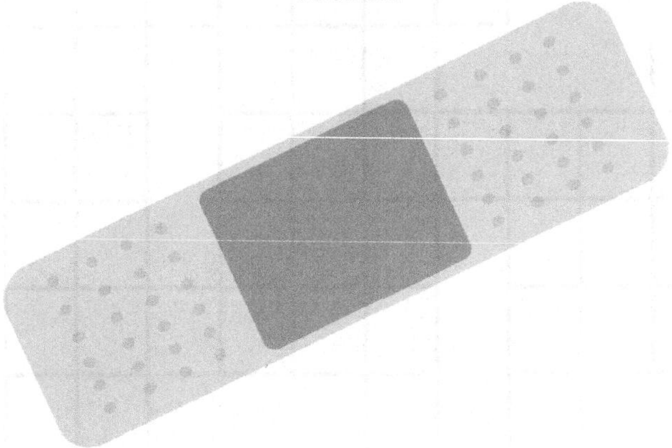

```
M V L U C I T E T H E R M O S E L
A A U O L I L O D P T X V C I X J
T U G A B E N N I E I T L O C R W
N P E I S N O C A T L T X O R E X
A S R K C V W X D I L C O M R F B
L S T L R M B C N T E F L O N A P
Y C K E A H A D A I T H A O J O Y
M O E E B W D R B Q S W A E R L R
S T E N B U Z U K E X N M Z M O E
P C V E L C R O R E P E R S P E X
A H H X E E F V G A R O L A I D S
M T G O R T E X V V L N U I T V K
C A R B O L O Y E E A U O U S E N
A P A H Z V Q I N V A R M L D W C
Y E M V I Y E L L A L S S I R I C
M E C C A N O R D V U K Z P N O X
M A S O N I T E M A O F O R Y T S
```

					6			2
					4			
			5	9	2	4		1
7	3						6	
6			2	1		5		
		9						
	8				1			3
				8			4	6
2			7					8

SUDOKU 18 - HARD

6						5		
						6		3
7		9		8	6			
	1				8		4	
				7				
			2	6			8	1
		6	9					
	7						2	
4		2				9		

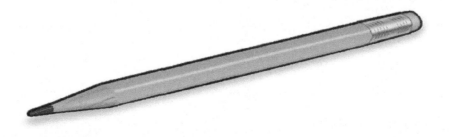

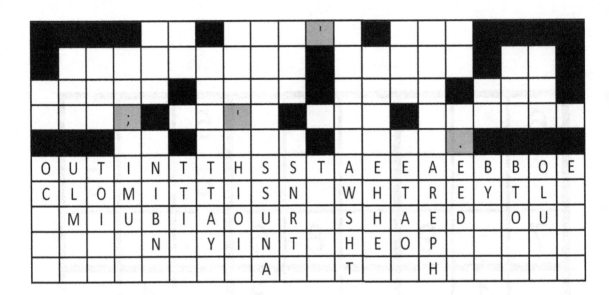

Dumb Joke...

How do fish get high?

(answer on page 110)

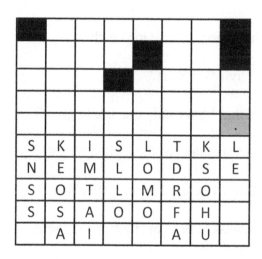

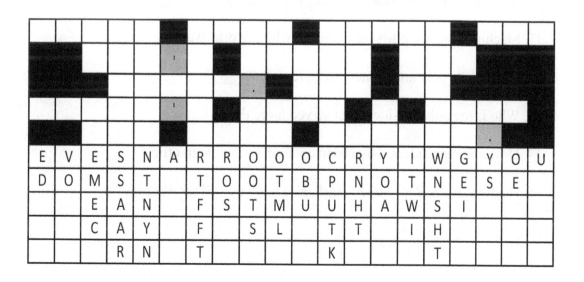

USA HISTORY TRIVIA QUESTIONS

How well do you know USA History? Take the quiz below to find out!

1. Who said "Give me liberty or give me death?" _____

2. What year did the Civil War Start? _____

3. Who said, "I regret that I have only one life to give for my country?" _____

4. Who was the second president of the United States? _____

5. The Battle of the Bulge occurred during what War? _____

6. How many amendments to the Constitution are there? _____

7. How many branches of the US Government are there? _____

8. Who was the first U.S. president to appear on television? _____

9. What year did Congress pass the right of woman to vote? _____

10. True or False? American currency is backed by gold. _____

11. Machine guns were first used during which World War? _____

12. What is the only amendment to be repealed? _____

13. Who is the only president that served more than 2 terms? _____

14. How many presidents have been assassinated while in office? _____

15. What year was Wall Street Crash, also known as Black Tuesday? _____

a. Franklin Delano Roosevelt

b. 1

c. Patrick Henry

d. 1919

e. 4

f. Franklin Roosevelt

g. Nathan Hale

h. 2

i. 27

j. 3

k. 1861

l. false

m. 18

n. 1929

o. John Adams

1...c, 2...k, 3...g, 4...o, 5...h, 6...i, 7...j, 8...f, 9...d, 10...l, 11...b, 12...m, 13...a, 14...e, 15...n

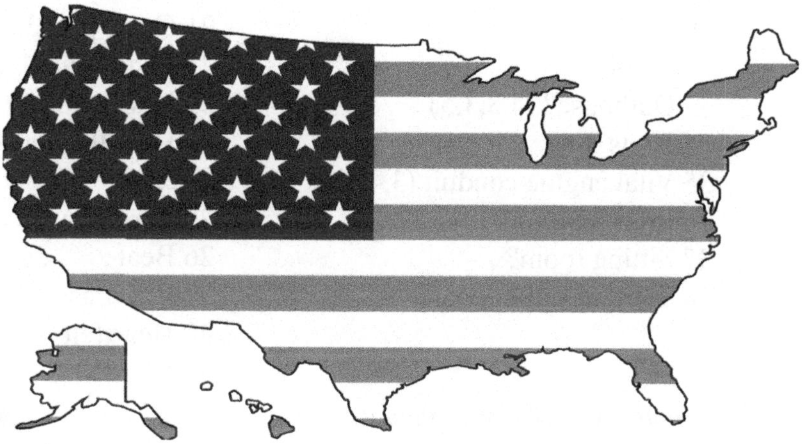

CROSSWORD 10

Across

2 No-show
6 Had a tiger for a shipmate
7 Hair salon stock
9 Office stations
10 Ltr. holder
12 Circus Hall of Fame site
14 "Absolutely!"
17 Do, re, mi
18 Relief
19 Carpentry tool
20 Animation
22 Somehow (3,3,2,7)
27 Lousy
28 Witch
29 Fib
31 Extol
33 Outhouse? (4,3,3,5)
34 Poets' feet
35 Vital engine conduit (3,4)
36 Improvise (4,2)
37 Sitting room?
38 They're full of beans

Down

1 Special delivery?
2 Mar, in a way
3 But, to Brutus
4 Quit
5 Failing grades
6 Ballpoint, e.g.
7 Pay (up)
8 Tiara wearer (4,7)
10 Book after Proverbs: Abbr.
11 Swerve
13 Duct opening?
15 Buffalo's AAA baseball team
16 Send to the canvas
20 Battery units
21 Quip, part 2
22 Fuddy-duddy (3-9)
23 Not permanent
24 How this answer is situated (5,2,4)
25 Spring event (5,6)
26 Beat
29 Big brass
30 Heartfelt
32 Rattle

(numbers at the end of clues indicate multiple word answer and their letter count)

WORD FIND 10 - VEGETABLES

bean
beet
broccoli
caper
capsicum
carrot
celeriac
celery
chard
chicory
chili
chive
cole
corn
cos lettuce
courgette
cress
endive
eschalot
fitch
giant shallot
gourd
kale
King Edward
leek
lentil
maize

nettle
okra
onion
parsnip
pea
plantain
potato
pulse
radish
red pepper
sage
soy
swede
tomato
turnip
yam

```
E W X F Y T C O D P L A N T A I N
T C Y R S M O R A D I S H U V Z M
D O A R F A L L P U L S E C T X L
R O R P E Y E C A O E S E A O T E
A T C R S L H K H H T T L P L X E
H A C E A I E Y I I C A T E L A K
C M X R L C C C M N V S T R A S D
E O H I E E M U O O G E E O H C R
D T S C S S R C M I T E N P S H E
I R T L T W S I U N R N D M T I P
L F O E E I E H A O I D A W N C P
I B Z S G T F D Y C A I Y T A O E
T D A H B R T R E R Z V B E I R P
N G B Y E R U U K E C E S E G Y D
E Q J O A B R O C C O L I B Z H E
L K O S N E M G C E T U R N I P R
P I N S R A P Z A W P C O R N B K
```

5			8	4				
							2	6
	3		9			4		1
		9		1	8	6		
7	5							8
							4	9
				7		2		
		6						3
			2		9	1		

	6		2			5		3
						9		1
3		5	9					
	9			6		4	8	
		2			4			5
5				7				
4								
	8				7	2	4	9

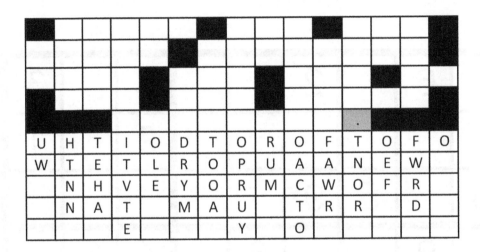

U	H	T	I	O	D	T	O	R	O	F	T	O	F	O
W	T	E	T	L	R	O	P	U	A	A	N	E	W	
	N	H	V	E	Y	O	R	M	C	W	O	F	R	
	N	A	T		M	A	U		T	R	R		D	
			E			Y			O					

Dumb Joke...

What is the dumbest animal in the jungle?

(answer on page 110)

FALLEN QUOTES 29, 30

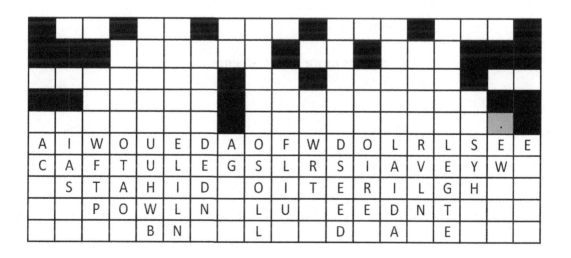

FIND SOMEONE WHO....

Communicating with other people is proven to improve overall health. See if you can find someone who... Score a point for every one you find!

_____ owns more than three pets.

_____ takes baths instead of showers.

_____ has visited more than 5 countries.

_____ has made beer.

_____ speaks more than 2 languages.

_____ does not like broccoli.

_____ who has been in a play.

_____ has had their tonsils removed.

_____ sings in a choir.

_____ who has more than 5 siblings.

May the road rise up to meet you.
May the wind be always at your back.
May the sun shine warm upon your face.
And rains fall soft upon your fields.
And until we meet again,
May God hold you in the hollow of His hand.

Irish Blessing

Crossword 1 - page 3

Crossword 2 - page 13

Crossword 3 - page 23

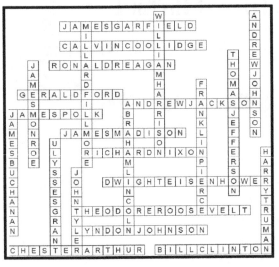

Crossword 4 - page 33

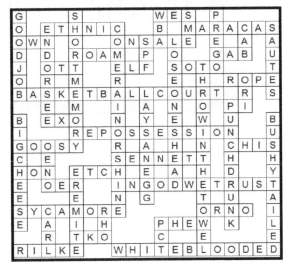

Crossword 5 - page 43

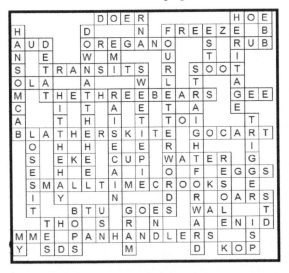

Crossword 6 - page 53

Crossword 7 - page 63

Crossword 8 - page 73

Crossword 9 - page 83

Crossword 10 - page 93

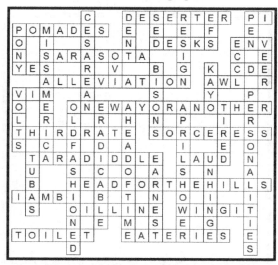

Word Find 1 - page 5

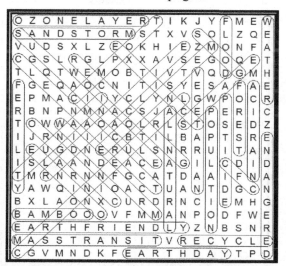

Word Find 2 - page 15

Word Find 3 - page 25

Word Find 4 - page 35

Word Find 5 - page 45

Word Find 6 - page 55

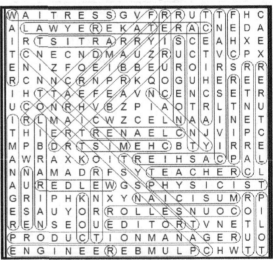

Word Find 7 - page 65

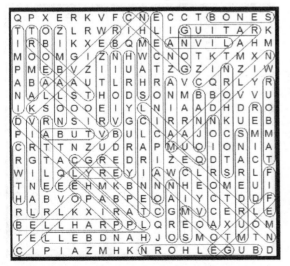

Word Find 8 - page 75

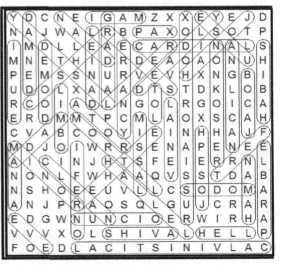

Word Find 9 - page 85

Word Find 10 - page 95

Sudoku 1 - page 6

3	6	9	7	2	8	1	4	5
7	2	1	4	9	5	3	6	8
8	4	5	1	6	3	9	7	2
1	5	2	6	7	9	4	8	3
6	9	3	8	5	4	7	2	1
4	7	8	2	3	1	5	9	6
9	1	4	3	8	2	6	5	7
5	8	6	9	1	7	2	3	4
2	3	7	5	4	6	8	1	9

Sudoku 2 - page 7

7	4	8	3	2	6	9	1	5
3	9	5	8	4	1	2	6	7
6	1	2	7	5	9	3	4	8
9	5	7	2	1	4	6	8	3
4	8	1	6	3	7	5	2	9
2	6	3	5	9	8	4	7	1
1	7	4	9	6	5	8	3	2
5	3	6	1	8	2	7	9	4
8	2	9	4	7	3	1	5	6

Sudoku 3 - page 16

8	9	5	7	3	4	1	6	2
6	3	4	9	1	2	8	7	5
1	7	2	5	8	6	4	9	3
3	5	7	8	9	1	2	4	6
2	6	1	3	4	7	5	8	9
9	4	8	2	6	5	3	1	7
4	1	3	6	2	9	7	5	8
5	8	9	1	7	3	6	2	4
7	2	6	4	5	8	9	3	1

Sudoku 4 - page 17

3	5	1	6	7	9	4	2	8
9	8	2	1	5	4	6	3	7
6	7	4	2	8	3	9	1	5
2	4	5	3	9	8	7	6	1
7	9	6	5	1	2	3	8	4
8	1	3	7	4	6	5	9	2
5	2	7	9	6	1	8	4	3
4	3	9	8	2	5	1	7	6
1	6	8	4	3	7	2	5	9

Sudoku 5 - page 26

6	8	4	9	1	2	5	7	3
2	3	9	6	5	7	1	4	8
5	7	1	8	3	4	9	6	2
1	6	3	5	4	8	2	9	7
8	5	7	3	2	9	4	1	6
4	9	2	7	6	1	8	3	5
7	1	6	4	8	5	3	2	9
3	2	8	1	9	6	7	5	4
9	4	5	2	7	3	6	8	1

Sudoku 6 - page 27

3	7	4	8	9	2	5	1	6
8	5	2	4	1	6	9	3	7
6	9	1	7	3	5	8	2	4
2	1	9	6	4	3	7	8	5
7	3	5	9	2	8	6	4	1
4	8	6	5	7	1	2	9	3
9	2	7	3	5	4	1	6	8
1	4	8	2	6	7	3	5	9
5	6	3	1	8	9	4	7	2

Sudoku 7 - page 36

6	3	7	5	9	4	8	1	2
1	4	9	2	6	8	7	3	5
8	5	2	3	1	7	6	4	9
2	6	5	8	3	9	4	7	1
9	1	8	4	7	2	5	6	3
3	7	4	6	5	1	9	2	8
5	2	1	9	4	6	3	8	7
7	9	6	1	8	3	2	5	4
4	8	3	7	2	5	1	9	6

Sudoku 8 - page 37

3	7	6	8	1	4	5	9	2
4	8	1	5	9	2	3	7	6
2	9	5	7	3	6	4	1	8
7	6	2	3	4	8	1	5	9
1	5	4	9	2	7	8	6	3
8	3	9	1	6	5	2	4	7
5	4	8	2	7	9	6	3	1
6	1	7	4	8	3	9	2	5
9	2	3	6	5	1	7	8	4

Sudoku 9 - page 46

1	6	7	3	5	9	8	2	4
4	5	9	6	2	8	7	3	1
8	3	2	4	7	1	9	5	6
6	7	5	2	8	3	1	4	9
3	2	1	7	9	4	5	6	8
9	8	4	5	1	6	2	7	3
7	4	8	9	6	2	3	1	5
5	1	3	8	4	7	6	9	2
2	9	6	1	3	5	4	8	7

Sudoku 10 - page 47

2	3	6	1	8	7	4	5	9
4	8	7	5	9	2	3	1	6
9	5	1	3	6	4	7	8	2
5	4	9	8	1	6	2	3	7
7	1	8	2	3	9	6	4	5
3	6	2	4	7	5	1	9	8
8	2	4	6	5	1	9	7	3
6	9	5	7	4	3	8	2	1
1	7	3	9	2	8	5	6	4

Sudoku 11 - page 56

2	8	5	7	6	1	4	3	9
6	1	3	5	4	9	7	2	8
9	4	7	2	8	3	5	1	6
8	5	4	3	9	6	1	7	2
7	3	9	4	1	2	8	6	5
1	2	6	8	5	7	9	4	3
3	6	1	9	7	8	2	5	4
5	9	2	1	3	4	6	8	7
4	7	8	6	2	5	3	9	1

Sudoku 12 - page 57

7	9	8	1	6	3	4	5	2
6	5	4	7	8	2	1	3	9
1	3	2	4	5	9	8	7	6
5	6	7	3	4	8	9	2	1
8	1	9	2	7	6	3	4	5
4	2	3	9	1	5	6	8	7
2	7	1	8	9	4	5	6	3
9	8	6	5	3	7	2	1	4
3	4	5	6	2	1	7	9	8

Sudoku 13 - page 66

9	1	7	4	2	5	8	3	6
6	8	2	9	1	3	4	7	5
3	4	5	7	6	8	1	9	2
5	3	1	6	9	2	7	8	4
4	9	6	8	5	7	2	1	3
7	2	8	3	4	1	6	5	9
2	7	3	5	8	6	9	4	1
1	5	9	2	7	4	3	6	8
8	6	4	1	3	9	5	2	7

Sudoku 14 - page 67

2	7	9	5	3	8	4	1	6
4	8	5	1	6	9	7	3	2
6	1	3	4	2	7	5	9	8
7	5	8	2	1	6	3	4	9
3	4	2	8	9	5	6	7	1
9	6	1	7	4	3	8	2	5
1	3	6	9	8	4	2	5	7
8	2	7	3	5	1	9	6	4
5	9	4	6	7	2	1	8	3

Sudoku 15 - page 76

4	6	8	3	9	7	5	2	1
3	1	9	4	2	5	6	8	7
5	2	7	8	6	1	9	3	4
7	4	3	2	8	9	1	6	5
1	5	2	6	7	4	3	9	8
9	8	6	1	5	3	7	4	2
8	3	1	5	4	6	2	7	9
6	9	4	7	1	2	8	5	3
2	7	5	9	3	8	4	1	6

Sudoku 16 - page 77

5	8	1	6	4	7	2	9	3
7	3	4	2	1	9	8	6	5
6	9	2	8	5	3	1	4	7
2	5	9	4	8	1	7	3	6
4	6	7	5	3	2	9	8	1
8	1	3	9	7	6	5	2	4
9	2	5	7	6	4	3	1	8
1	4	8	3	9	5	6	7	2
3	7	6	1	2	8	4	5	9

Sudoku 17 - page 86

4	9	5	1	7	6	3	8	2
1	2	7	8	3	4	6	9	5
8	6	3	5	9	2	4	7	1
7	3	2	4	5	8	1	6	9
6	4	8	2	1	9	5	3	7
5	1	9	3	6	7	8	2	4
9	8	4	6	2	1	7	5	3
3	7	1	9	8	5	2	4	6
2	5	6	7	4	3	9	1	8

Sudoku 18 - page 87

6	4	3	7	2	1	5	9	8
1	2	8	4	5	9	6	7	3
7	5	9	3	8	6	4	1	2
2	1	7	5	9	8	3	4	6
8	6	4	1	7	3	2	5	9
3	9	5	2	6	4	7	8	1
5	8	6	9	4	2	1	3	7
9	7	1	6	3	5	8	2	4
4	3	2	8	1	7	9	6	5

Sudoku 19 - page 96

5	6	1	8	4	2	9	3	7
8	9	4	1	3	7	5	2	6
2	3	7	9	6	5	4	8	1
3	4	9	7	1	8	6	5	2
7	5	2	6	9	4	3	1	8
6	1	8	5	2	3	7	4	9
1	8	5	3	7	6	2	9	4
9	2	6	4	5	1	8	7	3
4	7	3	2	8	9	1	6	5

Sudoku 20 - page 97

9	6	1	2	4	8	5	7	3
8	2	4	7	5	3	9	6	1
3	7	5	9	1	6	8	2	4
7	9	3	1	6	5	4	8	2
6	1	2	8	9	4	7	3	5
5	4	8	3	7	2	1	9	6
2	3	9	4	8	1	6	5	7
4	5	7	6	2	9	3	1	8
1	8	6	5	3	7	2	4	9

Quote Falls 1,2,3 - page 8, 9

1 - People say nothing is impossible, but I do nothing every day.

2 - Life is ten percent what happens to you and ninety percent how you react to it.

3 - My ex-girlfriend still misses me. But her aim is steadily improving.

Quote Falls 4,5,6 - page 18, 19

4 - I always wanted to be somebody, but now I realize I should have been more specific.

5 - If you are going through hell...keep going.

6 - If at first you don't succeed, you should not try skydiving.

Quote Falls 7,8,9 - page 28, 29

7 - If you are lonely dim the lights and put on a horror movie. Soon it won't feel like you are alone anymore.

8 - I would rather attempt to do something great and fail than to attempt nothing and succeed.

9 - Time flies like an arrow. Fruit flies like a banana.

Quote Falls 10, 11, 12 - page 38, 39

10 - Hope is being able to see that there is light despite all of the darkness.

11 - I wish everything in life was as easy as getting fat.

12 - I told the doctor I broke my leg in two places. He told me to quit going to those places.

Quote Falls 13, 14, 15 - page 48, 49

13 - If you think you are too small to make a difference, try sleeping with a mosquito.

14 - Every strike brings me closer to the next home run.

15 - Most folks are about as happy as they make their minds up to be.

Quote Falls 16, 17, 18- page 58, 59

16 - Success is going from failure to failure without losing your enthusiasm.

17 - Even if you fall on your face, you are still moving forward.

18 - It is not happiness that makes us grateful, but the gratefulness that makes us happy.

Quote Falls 19, 20, 21 - page 68, 69

19 - The only way to happiness is to cease worrying about things which are beyond the power of our will.

20 - The great essentials for happiness in this life are something to do, something to love and something to hope for.

21 - No one has ever become poor by giving.

Quote Falls 22, 23, 24- page 78, 79

22 - Let me not beg for the stilling of my pain, but for the heart to conquer it.

23 - All the art of living lies in a fine mingling of letting go and holding on.

24 - You can move through life seeing nothing as a miracle, or seeing everything as a miracle.

Quote Falls 25, 26, 27- page 88, 89

25 - It isn't the mountains ahead to climb that wear you out; it's the pebble in your shoe.

26 - Smooth seas do not make skillful sailors.

27 - Every fool knows you can't touch the stars, but it doesn't stop a wise man from trying.

Quote Falls 28, 29, 30- page 98, 99

28 - Never put off until tomorrow what you can do the day after tomorrow.

29 - If you can't do great things, do small things in a great way.

30 - If we all did the things we are capable of doing we would literally astound ourselves.

Joke Answers

page 58 - snowballs

page 68 - gummi bears

page 78 - buy a deck of cards

page 88 - seaweed

page 98 - the polar bear

Made in the USA
Monee, IL
25 September 2023

43382969R00063